An Apathetic Empath

By Danah Valeré

Published by Danah Valeré

ISBN 9798387864995

Published by Danah Valeré
danahvalere@gmail.com
Engage at: www.youtube.com/danahvalere
and danah_valere@Instagram

Thank You's:

I'd like to thank the Zakers family, in whose home I wrote the first draft of this endeavor.
I'd like to thank Alvin Munson for insisting (for decades) that my poetry was ready to publish.
I'd like to thank the Infinite Wisdom Seekers book club for reading, listening, and encouraging.
Thank you, Sanaa Saddiqi, for your most valuable feedback.
And I'd like to thank all my family and friends for their support over the years, especially my mother, for teaching me poems before any nursery rhyme and filling my heart with books.

Danah Valeré

Danah Valeré

How to Read this Book:

This collection is a story consisting of many stories. First of all, pieces of a comic, which weave together to form the macrocosmic version of the story (or summary), can be found on the illustrated pages. And behind most illustrated pages is a set of poems that matches the energy of the illustration before it. Each poem is a story, too, a slither of time, a moment, in a greater narrative. Some poems are accompanied by bonus content accessed via the QR code in the upper right corner. There, you may also engage in the comments section of a video, like it, and share it. Welcome, tribe, I've been waiting for you.

Danah Valeré

Danah Valeré

Table of Contents

A beginning
is just the death
of some old shit.
R.I.P.
Beloved

An Apathetic Empath

[To a Young Tree]

She broke through the dirt like a tree—
wimpy, at first.
The wind could shake her,
the rain could drown her,
some rat could use her
to sharpen his teeth.
And they did.
Wimpy—she was wimpy!
But she lived,
so she grew.

Then she fought to the sky—
uncertain... certainly.
The sun could burn her,
other trees could block her,
some bird could rip out her limbs.
And they did.
Uncertain—she was so unsure of herself!
But she lived,
so she grew.

Getting taller—
she grew.
Getting fatter—
she grew.
Getting stronger—
she grew.

Until...

She kissed other leaves in the canopy—
shyly, at first.
Silence could shame her.
A nudge could scare her.
Some stranger could make her forget her roots.
And they did.
Shy—*backwardly* bashful.
But she lived.
So, she grew.

An Apathetic Empath

[Spoken Word]

Open—
my mind—
like a cannister of soggy spaghetti-o's.
I have been premature—
my tastes unrefined—
throwing temper tantrums,
like red sauce,
on the walls of a preliterate art form.
"Follow the ooo's!" I stamped my foot.
But they would not.
They demanded my voice
and ripped it from my rhythmic heart,
then danced in the dissonance
of blood gurgling in my song.
I shake.
I cry—
unused to being naked.
I want to hide behind the page
like an absent academic,
but the people would not have it.
My mouth was torn ajar.

And a wise woman
once said,
"If it's not growing,
it's dead."
R.I.P.

An Apathetic Empath

Nah-uh.

[Ink Splatters]

a pause
a silence in the noise
a hiccup that lasts a while
a *long* while
forever while
epiphany-of-past-shitty-deeds while

I *long* for the noise
the rush of unwanted chatter and automatic thoughts
I cry out with my pen,
scratch bleached papyrus with a sharp edge

it's not edgy enough
sounds like everything else that's ever been screamed
in ink

I scry in my veins
the coming and going

damn
I really don't want peace

I'd rather
transcribe the static in my mind
sell it
and watch people consume it
the electrifying roar I've been dying to vomit

... I've been *dying* to vomit?
I ask myself

yet no ink
splatters
here

An Apathetic Empath

[Lumen]

How can I explain the light
that creeps in from
my window?
Dark and subtle, at first,
like the single cousin
who's always
just a guest
at the wedding,
at the last table,
in the last chair,
two sniffs from the restroom—
an afterthought.
It creeps in like that—
like its bangs are too low
and its eyes don't know
how to look at anything
but its own toes.
Dark—
but only in the eyes,
that's how this morning feels.
It electrifies me
like the beauty
only God can see
in a downcast girl.
This dawn
is the turning of a key
like the knob-less rods
on a gas stove
in a walk-up on three.
And like the hiss and the scent
before the flame
is fully lit,
that space between the metal
and where the sparks fly—
that,
that's today's sunrise,
cloudy and sputtering
and full of potential
like the girl
at the last table at the wedding
approaching the party
too shy
to let her shoes clack.
And just like that,
before anyone knows what's happened,
she catches fire
and
illuminates the room.

An Apathetic Empath

[Fuji]

we are in the side of the mountain
everywhere is mountain
and water
and green
a tiny train twinkles silently
far off in the dark
boats twinkle
parties twinkle
in rich homes on the highest mounds
the mastery of life carries in their voices
we are thrilled to be here
we're not normal anymore
we have bought a disappearing share
in the hot, misty air
on Fuji
the bourgeois dance
at their fully stocked bars
on the tippy-*toest* point
of the highest mounds
under deified stars
and we dance with our tiny liquor bottles
on our tippy, tippy toes
on a very low mound
as if we're masters, too
we borrow the sounds of their djs
their permissions not needed
we are free from our vulgar prisons
and our mundane existences back home
we cackle while passing signs we can't read
we are skipping in a dream
under the streetlights
under the treetops
under the mountain pinnacle
under the glimmering gods in a dark, navy sky
may we never forget Mount Fuji

An Apathetic Empath

[These Rivers]

It's been raining all day,
but I haven't really noticed.
I've been tuned in
and dialed up
and working like a swollen tit,
when *I just wanna be free*
(this quarantine's
been the best thing
for me),
but I guess I have to cross that river, first.

It's been so quiet;
I've had time to think.
I've been spread
on my bed naked
savoring a long blink.
And though I'm fulfilled by my work,
soul searching's more filling.
Eye need to be free to see,
but I've gotta cross this river, first.

So, hear me, river—
turbulent wisdom-giver,
be my guide and not my foe.
Bless the ish I've got to swim through
just to prove
I deserve more.

Can I face my fears and demons?
Can I wrestle with my greatness?
Can I fight through all my weaknesses
to become my very best?
The river is the test.
Either swallow me
or quench my thirst.
I'm thrashing t'ward a dream,
and I have to cross these rivers, first.

So, I'm looking at things
more closely now.

An Apathetic Empath

[LOUD]

Morning crawls beneath her skin
she stirs
blinks
the dark swaddles her
she throws back the comforter
toes on the frozen tile
sits her bottom
on the comfy couch
earbuds in
music
LOUD!

An Apathetic Empath

[Inner Cherub]

Sifting through my thoughts,
turning down my inner noise,
I lay my body down again
and *this* time, I listen.

And like a shy waif,
she suddenly appears,
bent back at the waist,
her hair upon her ears.
She's toeing her own toes,
hands tucked behind her tightly,
chin to chest and breasts to nose,
big eyes looking *out of me*.

"You promised we would dream tonight.
You promise every night.
But rarely do you come with me.
***Will** we dream tonight?"*

And though I *often*
break my word to me
to give it to the world,
still she offers me forgiveness,
her vision, and her secrets.

An Apathetic Empath

[Twinkie]

He's a twinkie—
sugar, dye,
and every nonperishable trick in the book.

He leaves women bogged down with baggage
like a twinkie leaves fat
on the flanks of famished girls.

To love him
is to sign a blank check
to a dick
for a twinkie.

Empty calories.
Major consequences.

An Apathetic Empath

[Dance!]

I'm of use to you now.
You didn't love me before,
treat me like a co-creator,
repay my smile with your smile,
or greet me warmly in a frosty morning.

But *now*
you stare at me with your teeth out,
eyes cocked open,
searching for the keys to my submission,
listening, finally,
as if they jangled in my voice.
You mean to flatter me.
You mean to stroke me.
You mean to use me as a tool;
I mind.

I'm of use to you now.
Damn being bashful.
You don't even hold back
anymore.
You see a pearl
twisted deep,
bound to my ribs,
pulsing,
and, boldly, you mean to get it.

A part of me welcomes your advance,
giver that I am.

Oh, but *this* time,
you *will*
dance for it!

And I see a lot of dead MFs
just walking around.

An Apathetic Empath

[Classico Romantico]

Love your own time.
Admiration of the distant past
is only an escape—
an illusion that wouldn't last
if one took the pain
of living then.

Perhaps, travel
to remember how
it feels to be misplaced—
in the new Now
the universe unravels
and you could be in any when.

Here, we sit,
our eyes focused on a slit
in the fabric of space-time—
now I get it
how I snubbed the *gift*.
The disenchanting present
is some one else's, "Back then!"

An Apathetic Empath

Not bad.
But I
wanted
better.

[AWAKE]

Wind in my face.
Eyes on the bumps before me.
An arousal
of carcinogenic fog
caught us unaware.
Mountains
of poisonous grey
thundered at us
like divine wool
to an interstate of *fleas*!
Orange danced
in the distance.
Yet, we moved forward
(thinking adults, capable
employees)
into the thick of it.
Zombies.
Our hearts slowed.
Our hands were steady on our steering wheels.
Our eyes—dead and gaping.
Some whispered, "It's *only* fog."
But we knew better…

What have we done?

An Apathetic Empath

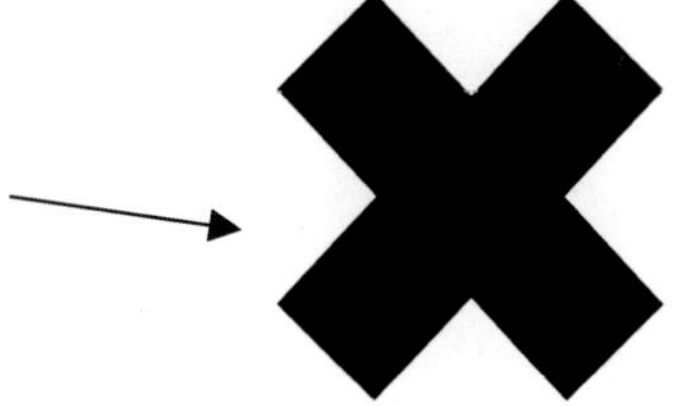

[Final Affairs]

Shall I burn
or suffocate?
I often wonder.
Shall I lie in a box
waiting to rot
while the decomposed folks
spread wings?

Or shall I fight through fire
to take to flight
faster,
rid my flesh like plaster
that traps some one in?

But what if I feel it?
What if I hear the blisters crisping;
and smell my hair melting
for what *seems* like eternity?

Do I embrace the fire?
Or lie below the rocks?

Shall I burn or shall I take the box?

An Apathetic Empath

[An Apathetic Empath]

she decided to have no feelings about it
there was nothing she could do about it anyway
and because everybody had their reasons for it
there was nothing they would do about it anyway

but she found
if she was really honest
and very, very still,
after slipping on the slippers of everyone else,
she didn't fully understand it no how
no one did

so, she tossed aside all the other shoes,
pealed off her damp socks,
and massaged the base
of her tortured toes,
placed her feet in her *own* soles,
then walked down the stairs, foot-happy,
into the quiet,
dim-lit kitchen
to eat a *box* of cereal

And love with them
is Impossible!

An Apathetic Empath

[I Know]

It's a ball above my navel
giving me the shivers
and a hot head
it's made of some metal
that conducts nervous energy
--you're avoiding me
I know

It spins in place
whirring and trembling
tearing the guts of the bearer
creating a crater
of ancient fear
--you're cheating me
I know

It's the shape
of emptiness
it's efficiency
catapults bolts
of *lovelessness*
through this body
--you're leaving me
I know

[To Hold and to Keep]

It would be nice
to sit beside someone
as I read
and I write
then lie
in an embrace
that lasts every night.
Pray.
Repeat
(same someone—
forever).

An Apathetic Empath

[Under the Palace Dragon]

I forgot about the Koi fish—
the way they *really* see you,
each flailing to the top
of the school
just to meet you,
under the palace dragon,
under a blue, white sky.

I sat on a stone
littered with cherry blossoms.
My legs like the wings of a butterfly,
I teased the Koi fish
and dreamt of you.

The palace wrapped
around my reverie,
shielding me
from the busy world outside.
A dragon rested
along its walls,
demanding peace,
but daring chaos.

I
sat on a wet stone
littered with cherry blossoms.
My legs like the wings of a butterfly,
I teased the Koi fish
but remembered you.
Under the place dragon.
Under a clear white sky.

An Apathetic Empath

[His Love'll Be Enough]

I've been on the tops of towers
with handsome men
while drinking spirits.
I've looked down
on the tiny world
through glass floors.
I've had women
whose eyes would not meet mine
gingerly clean up after me,
and men
who made the world spin 'round
admit I was too much for them.
I'm alone
because I'm tired
of pretending my wings are clipped
when *others* cannot fly,
of pretending
my brain is filled with daffodils,
or that my legs could open
when my heart is closed.
I'm exhausted.
Bearing your seeds
is not enough for me.
And this...
this is not an emancipation proclamation
of the softer side of man.
I don't *want* to be free of you.
I want to nestle my nose in your chest
and only stir to bring you coffee.
I wanna bring you lemonade
after you mow the lawn,
beer when you watch the game,
then let you love me
at the end of the day.
But I can't do these things,
leave myself exposed,
fall...
if you won't catch me.
So, lay your palms over my breasts...
one last time.
Ignore the erratic beating of my heart.
It's only lying to my mind
as my body lies in your spoon,
saying,
"Soon,
pugh-pugh,
soon,
his love'll be enough,
pugh-pugh,
soon.
Pugh-pugh,
pugh-pugh..."

An Apathetic Empath

[A Woman on Love]

I love until I'm tired of loving
just as I'll live until I'm done
'cause what else is there to do?
I'm only a woman

and I'll smile 'till I'm done
just like I welcome you
'till I can't stand forgiving

because I'm a woman
and that's how it's done

I'll love and live
and live and love
until I am
and love

no one.

So, here's
to
new
beginnings!